SCHIRMER'S LIBRARY
OF MUSICAL CLASSICS

FREDERIC CHOPIN

Complete Works for the Piano

Edited and Fingered,
and provided with an Introductory Note by
CARL MIKULI

Historical and Analytical Comments by
JAMES HUNEKER

ISBN 978-0-7935-5200-9

G. SCHIRMER, Inc.

DISTRIBUTED BY

HAL•LEONARD
CORPORATION
7777 W. BLUEMOUND RD. P.O. BOX 13819 MILWAUKEE, WI 53213

FRÉDÉRIC FRANÇOIS CHOPIN

According to a tradition—and, be it said, an erroneous one—Chopin's playing was like that of one dreaming rather than awake—scarcely audible in its continual *pianissimos* and *una cordas*, with feebly developed technique and quite lacking in confidence, or at least indistinct, and distorted out of all rhythmic form by an incessant *tempo rubato!* The effect of these notions could not be otherwise than very prejudicial to the interpretation of his works, even by the most able artists—in their very striving after truthfulness; besides, they are easily accounted for.

Chopin played rarely and always unwillingly in public; "exhibitions" of himself were totally repugnant to his nature. Long years of sickliness and nervous irritability did not always permit him the necessary repose in the concert-hall, for displaying untrammeled the full wealth of his resources. In more familiar circles, too, he seldom played anything but his shorter pieces, or occasional fragments from the larger works. Small wonder, therefore, that Chopin the Pianist should fail of general recognition.

Yet Chopin possessed a highly developed technique, giving him complete mastery over the instrument. In all styles of touch the evenness of his scales and passages was unsurpassed—nay, fabulous; under his hands the pianoforte needed to envy neither the violin for its bow nor wind-instruments for the living breath. The tones melted one into the other with the liquid effect of beautiful song.

A genuine piano-hand, extremely flexible though not large, enabled him to play arpeggios of most widely dispersed harmonies and passages in wide stretches, which he brought into vogue as something never attempted before; and everything without the slightest apparent exertion, a pleasing freedom and lightness being a distinguishing characteristic of his style. At the same time, the tone which he could *draw out* of the instrument was prodigious, especially in the *cantabiles;* in this regard John Field alone could compare with him.

A lofty, virile energy lent imposing effect to suitable passages—an energy without roughness; on the other hand, he could carry away his hearers by the tenderness of his soulful delivery—a tenderness without affectation. But with all the warmth of his peculiarly ardent temperament, his playing was always within bounds, chaste, polished and at times even severely reserved.

In keeping time Chopin was inflexible, and many will be surprised to learn that the metronome never left his piano. Even in his oft-decried *tempo rubato* one hand—that having the accompaniment—always played on in strict time, while the other, singing the melody, either hesitating as if undecided, or, with increased animation, anticipating with a kind of impatient vehemence as if in passionate utterances, maintained the freedom of musical expression from the fetters of strict regularity.

Some information concerning Chopin the Teacher, even in the shape of a mere sketch, can hardly fail to interest many readers.

Far from regarding his work as a teacher, which his position as an artist and his social connections in Paris rendered difficult of avoidance, as a burdensome task, Chopin daily devoted his entire energies to it for several hours and with genuine delight. True, his demands on the talent and industry of the pupil were very great. There were often "de leçons orageuses" ("stormy lessons"), as they were called in school parlance, and many a fair eye wet with tears departed from the high altar of the Cité d'Orleans, rue St. Lazare, yet without the slightest resentment on that score against the dearly beloved master. For this same severity, so little prone to easy satisfaction, this feverish vehemence with which the master strove to raise his disciples to his own plane, this insistence on the repetition of a passage until it was understood, were a guaranty that he had the pupil's progress at heart. He would glow with a sacred zeal for art; every word from his lips was stimulating and inspiring. Single lessons often lasted literally for several hours in succession, until master and pupil were overcome by fatigue.

On beginning with a pupil, Chopin was chiefly anxious to do away with any stiffness in, or cramped, convulsive movement of, the hand, thereby obtaining the first requisite of a fine technique, "souplesse" (suppleness), and at the same time independence in the motion of the fingers. He was never tired of inculcating that such technical exercises are not merely mechanical, but claim the intelligence and entire will-power of the pupil: and, consequently, that a twentyfold or fortyfold repetition (still the lauded arcanum of so many schools) does no good whatever—not to mention the kind of practising advocated by Kalkbrenner, during which one may also occupy oneself with reading! He treated the various styles of touch very thoroughly, more especially the full-toned *legato.*

As gymnastic aids he recommended bending the wrist inward and outward, the repeated wrist-stroke, the pressing apart of the fingers—but all with an earnest warning against over-exertion. For scale-practice he required a very full tone, as *legato* as possible, at first very slowly and taking a quicker tempo only step by step, and playing with metronomic evenness. To facilitate the passing under of the thumb and passing over of the fingers, the hand was to be bent inward. The scales having many black keys (B major, F-sharp, D-flat) were studied first, C major, as the hardest, coming last. In like order he took up Clementi's Preludes and Exercises, a work which he highly valued on account of its utility. According to Chopin, evenness in scale-playing and arpeggios depends not only on the equality in the strength of the fingers obtained through five-finger exercises, and a perfect freedom of the thumb in passing under and over, but foremostly on the perfectly smooth and constant sideways movement of the hand (not *step* by *step*), letting the elbow hang down freely and loosely at all times. This movement he exemplified by a *glissando* across the keys. After this he gave as studies a selection from Cramer's Études, Clementi's Gradus ad Parnassum, The Finishing Studies in Style by Moscheles, which were very congenial to him, Bach's English and French Suites, and some Preludes and Fugues from the Well-Tempered Clavichord.

Field's and his own nocturnes also figured to a certain extent as studies, for through them—partly by learning from his explanations, partly by hearing and imitating them as played indefatigably by Chopin himself—the pupil was taught to recognize, love and produce the *legato* and the beautiful connected singing tone. For paired notes and chords he exacted strictly simultaneous striking of the notes; an arpeggio being permitted only where marked by the composer himself; in the trill, which he generally commenced on the auxiliary, he required perfect evenness rather than great rapidity, the closing turn to be played easily and without haste.

For the turn (*gruppetto*) and appoggiatura he recommended the great Italian singers as models; he desired octaves to be played with the wrist-stroke, but without losing in fullness of tone thereby. Only far-advanced pupils were given his Études Op. 10 and Op. 25.

Chopin's attention was always directed to teaching correct phrasing. With reference to wrong phrasing he often repeated the apt remark, that it struck him as if some one were reciting, in a language not understood by the speaker, a speech carefully learned by rote, in the course of which the speaker not only neglected the natural quantity of the syllables, but even stopped in the middle of words. The pseudo-musician, he said, shows in a similar way, by his wrong phrasing, that music is not his mother-tongue, but something foreign and incomprehensible to him, and must, like the aforesaid speaker, quite renounce the idea of making any effect upon his hearers by his delivery.

In marking the fingering, especially that peculiar to himself, Chopin was not sparing. Piano-playing owes him many innovations in this respect, whose practicalness caused their speedy adoption, though at first certain authorities, like Kalkbrenner, were fairly horrified by them. For example, Chopin did not hesitate to use the thumb on the black keys, or to pass it under the little finger (with a decided inward bend of the wrist, to be sure), where it facilitated the execution, rendering the latter quieter and smoother. With one and the same finger he often struck two neighboring keys in succession (and this not simply in a slide from a black key to the next white one), without the slightest noticeable break in the continuity of the tones. He frequently passed the longest fingers over each other without the intervention of the thumb (see Étude No. 2, Op. 10), and not only in passages where (e.g.) it was made necessary by the holding down of a key with the thumb. The fingering for chromatic thirds based on this device (and marked by himself in Étude No. 5, Op. 25), renders it far easier to obtain the smoothest *legato* in the most rapid tempo, and with a perfectly quiet hand, than the fingering followed before. The fingerings in the present edition are, in most cases, those indicated by Chopin himself; where this is not the case, they are at least marked in conformity with his principles, and therefore calculated to facilitate the execution in accordance with his conceptions.

In the shading he insisted on a real and carefully graduated *crescendo* and *decrescendo*. On phrasing, and on style in general, he gave his pupils invaluable and highly suggestive hints and instructions, assuring himself, however, that they were understood by playing not only single passages, but whole pieces, over and over again, and this with a scrupulous care, an enthusiasm, such as none of his auditors in the concert-hall ever had an opportunity to witness. The whole lesson-hour often passed without the pupil's having played more than a few measures, while Chopin, at a Pleyel upright piano (the pupil always played on a fine concert grand, and was obliged to promise to practise on only the best instruments), continually interrupting and correcting, proffered for his admiration and imitation the warm, living ideal of perfect beauty. It may be asserted, without exaggeration, that only the pupil knew Chopin the Pianist in his entire unrivalled greatness.

Chopin most urgently recommended ensemble-playing, the cultivation of the best chamber-music— but only in association with the finest musicians. In case no such opportunity offered, the best substitute would be found in four-hand playing.

With equal insistence he advised his pupils to take up thorough theoretical studies as early as practicable. Whatever their condition in life, the master's great heart always beat warmly for the pupils. A sympathetic, fatherly friend, he inspired them to unwearying endeavor, took unaffected delight in their progress, and at all times had an encouraging word for the wavering and dispirited.

CARL MIKULI.

THE NOCTURNES

HERE is the chronology of the Nocturnes: opus 9, three Nocturnes, January, 1833; opus 15, three Nocturnes, January, 1834; opus 27, two Nocturnes, May, 1836; opus 32, two Nocturnes, December, 1837; opus 37, two Nocturnes, May, 1840; opus 48, two Nocturnes, August, 1841; opus 55, two Nocturnes, August, 1844; opus 62, two Nocturnes, September, 1846. In addition there is a Nocturne written in 1828 and published by Fontana, with the opus number 72, No. 2, and one in C sharp minor, discovered later, written when Chopin was young, and published in 1895.

John Field has been described as the forerunner of Chopin. The limpid style of this pupil and friend of Clementi, and his beautiful touch and finished execution, were admired by the Pole. The nocturnes of Field are now neglected, though without warrant; not only is he the creator of the form, but in his nocturnes and concertos he has written sweet and sane music. Field rather patronized Chopin, with whose melancholy pose he had no patience. "He has a sick-room talent," growled the Irishman in the intervals between his wine-drinking, pipe-smoking, and the washing of his linen—the latter economical habit he had contracted from Clementi. There is some truth in this stricture. Chopin, seldom exuberantly cheerful, is in many of his Nocturnes morbidly sad and complaining. The most admired of his compositions, with the exception of his Waltzes, they are in several instances his weakest. Nevertheless, he ennobled the form originated by Field, giving it dramatic breadth, passion, even grandeur. Set agains' Field's naïve and idyllic specimens the efforts of Chopin are too often bejewelled, far too lugubrious, too tropical—Asiatic is a better word; and they have the exotic savor of the heated conservatory, not the fresh scent of the flowers grown in the open by the less poetic John Field. And then Chopin is so desperately sentimental at times. Some of these compositions are not altogether to the taste of the present generation; they seem anæmic in feeling. However, there are a few noble Nocturnes, and some methods of performance may have much to answer for in the sentimentalizing of the others. More vigor, a quickening of the time-pulse, and a less languishing touch, will rescue them from lush sentimentality. Chopin loved the night and its starry mysteries; his Nocturnes are true night-pieces, some wearing an agitated, remorseful countenance; others seen in profile only; while many are like whisperings at dusk—Verlaine moods. The poetic side of men of genius is feminine, and in Chopin the feminine note was over-emphasized, at moments it was almost hysterical, particularly in these Nocturnes. The Scotch have a proverb: "She wove her shroud and wore it in her lifetime." The shroud is not far away in the Nocturnes. Chopin wove his till the day of his death; and he sometimes wore it—but not always, as many persons believe.

Among the elegaic of his Nocturnes is the first in B flat minor; of far more significance than its two companions, it is, for some reason, neglected. While I am far from agreeing with those who hold that in the early Chopin his genius was completely revealed, yet this Nocturne is as striking as the last Nocturne; it is at once sensuous and dramatic, melancholy and lovely. Emphatically a gray mood. The section in octaves is exceedingly seductive. As a melody it contains all the mystic crooning and lurking voluptuousness of its composer. There is throughout flux and reflux, passion peeping out in the *coda*. The E flat Nocturne is graceful, shallow in content, but if it is played with purity of tone and freedom from sentimentalism it is not nearly as banal as it seems. It is Field-like, therefore play it, as did Rubinstein, in Field-like fashion. Hadow calls attention to the "remote and recondite modulations" in the twelfth bar, the chromatic double-notes. For him they are the only real modulation; "the rest of the passage is an iridescent play of color, an effect of superficies, not an effect of substance." It was the E flat Nocturne that unloosed Rellstab's critical wrath in the "Iris." Of it he wrote: "Where Field smiles, Chopin makes a grinning grimace; where Field sighs, Chopin groans," and so on, a string of antitheses, witty but irrelevant, ending with the rather comical plea: "We implore Mr. Chopin to return to nature." Rellstab might have added that, while Field is often commonplace, Chopin never is. Gracious, even coquettish, is the first part of the B major Nocturne of this opus. Well knit, the passionate intermezzo has the true dramatic ring. It should be taken *alla breve*. The ending is quite effective.

I do not care very much for the F major Nocturne. This opus 15 is dedicated to Ferdinand Hiller. Ehlert speaks of "the ornament in triplets with which he brushes the theme as with the gentle wings of a butterfly," and then discusses the artistic value of the ornament which may be so profitably studied in the Chopin music. "From its nature, the ornament can only beautify the beautiful." Music like Chopin's, with its predominating elegance, could not forgo ornament.

Ehlert thinks that the F sharp major Nocturne is inseparable from champagne and truffles. It is more elegant, also more dramatic than the one in F major, which precedes it. That, with the exception of the middle part in F minor, is weak, though pretty and confiding. The F sharp major Nocturne is popular. The *doppio movimento* is extremely striking, the entire piece saturated with young life, love and feeling of good-will to mankind. The third Nocturne of this opus is in G minor and exhibits picturesque writing. There is not much of the fantastic, yet the languid earth-weary voice of the opening and the churchly refrain of the chorale—is there not here fantastic contrast! This Nocturne contains in solution all that Chopin developed in a later Nocturne of the same key. I think the first stronger, its lines simpler, more primitive, its coloring less varied, yet quite as rich and gloomy. Of it Chopin on being interrogated for its key said: "After Hamlet," but changing his mind added, "Let them guess for themselves." A sensible conclusion. Kullak's programme is conventional. It is the lament for the beloved one, the lost Lenore, with religious consolation thrown in as a make-weight. The bell-tones of the plain-chant evoke for me little that is consoling, though the piece ends in the major mode. It is more like Poe's "Ulalume." A tiny tone-poem, Anton Rubinstein made much of it. In the seventeenth bar and during four bars there is a held note, F, and I once heard the Russian virtuoso keep this tone prolonged by some miraculous means. The *tempo* is very slow, and the tone is not in a position where the sustaining pedal can sensibly help it. Yet under Rubinstein's velvet fingers it swelled and diminished, and went on singing into the E as if the instrument were an organ. I suppose the inaudible changing of fingers on the note, with his artistic pedalling, achieved the wonderful effect.

The next Nocturne, opus 27, No. 1, brings us to a masterpiece. With the possible exception of the C minor Nocturne, this one in the sombre key of C sharp minor is a great essay in the form. Kleczynski finds it "a description of a calm night at Venice, where, after a scene of murder, the sea closes over a corpse and continues to mirror the moonlight"; which is melodramatic. The wide-meshed figure of the left hand supports a morbid, persistent melody that grates on the nerves. From the *più mosso* the agitation increases, and just here note the Beethovenish quality of these bars, which continues till the change of key-signature. There is a surprising climax followed by sunshine in the D flat part; then, after mounting dissonances, a bold succession of octaves leads to the feverish plaint of the opening. The composition attains exalted states; its psychologic tension is at times so great as to lead the hearer to the border of the pathologic. There is fantastic power in this Nocturne, which is seldom interrupted with sinister subtlety. Henry T. Finck rightfully

believes it "embodies a greater variety of emotion and more genuine dramatic spirit on four pages than many operas on four hundred." The companion picture in D flat, opus 27, No. 2, has, as Karasowski writes, "a profusion of delicate *fioriture.*" It contains but one subject and is an intimate song; there is obvious meaning in the duality of voices. Often heard in the concert room, this Nocturne gives us a surfeit of thirds and sixths in elaborate ornamentation, and a certain monotone of mood; and it is an imploring melody, harmonically interesting. A curious marking in the older editions, and usually overlooked by pianists, is the *crescendo* and *con forza* of the little cadenza. This is evidently erroneous. The theme should first be *piano*, and on its return *pianissimo* and *forte*, respectively, according to Kleczynski.

The best part of the next Nocturne—B major, opus 32, No. 1—is the *coda*; it is in minor and is like the drumbeat of tragedy. The entire ending, a stormy recitative, is in stern contrast to the dreamy beginning. The Nocturne that follows, in A flat, is a reversion to the Field type, the opening recalling that master's B flat major nocturne. The F minor section of Chopin's broadens out to dramatic reaches, but as an entirety this opus is not particularly noteworthy. The Nocturne in G minor, opus 37, No. 1, is much admired. The chorale, said Chopin's pupil. Gutmann, is taken too slowly, its composer having forgotten to mark the increased tempo. The Nocturne in G is exquisite. Painted with the most ethereal brush, without the cloying splendors of the D flat Nocturne, the double-thirds, fourths and sixths are magically euphonious. The second subject is one of the most beautiful penned by Chopin. It has the true barcarolle atmosphere, and subtle are the shifting harmonic hues. Pianists usually take the first part too fast, the second too slow, transposing the poetic composition into an agile étude. Both numbers of this opus are without dedications. They are the offspring of the trip to Majorca.

The Nocturne in C minor, opus 48, No. 1, has its despairing moments, but it is the broadest, most imposing and most dramatic of the series; its middle movement is a departure from the form. Biggest in conception, it is a miniature music-drama. Adequately to interpret it demands the grand manner. The *doppio movimento* is dramatically exciting. A fitting pendant is this composition to the C sharp minor Nocturne. Both works display the heroic quality, both are free from mawkishness, and are Chopin in the mode masculine. The following Nocturne No. 2, in F sharp minor, is poetic and contains a fine recitative in D flat. It was a favorite of its composer. Opus 55, two Nocturnes in F minor and E flat major, need no longer detain us. The first is familiar. Kleczynski devotes a page or more to its execution. He asks us to vary the return of the chief subject with nuances, as would an artistic singer the couplets of a classic song. There are "cries of despair" in it, but at last "a feeling of hope." It is the relief of a major key after prolonged wandering in the minor. Not epoch-making, it is a nice Nocturne, and neat in its sorrow. The succeeding example gives "the impression of an improvisation."

Opus 62 brings us to a pair in the respective keys of B and E major. The first, the so-called Tuberose Nocturne, is faint with a sickly, yet rich odor. The climbing trellis of notes that so unexpectedly leads to the tonic, is a fascinating surprise, and the chief tune has a fruity charm. The piece is highly ornate, its harmonies dense, the entire surface overruns with wild ornamentation and a profusion of trills. This Nocturne, the third of its kind in the key of B, is not easy; and though unduly luxuriant it deserves warmer praise than has been accorded it. Irregular as is its outline, its troubled lyrism is appealing, is melting, and the A flat portion with its timid, hesitating accents is very attractive. The following, the E major Nocturne, has the authentic Bardic ring. Its song is almost declamatory, the intermediate portion is both wavering and passionate. The work shows no decrease in creative vigor or lyric fancy. The posthumous Nocturne in E minor, composed in 1827, is rather pale yet sweet; it contains some very un-Chopinlike modulations. The C sharp minor, published two decades ago, is hardly a treasure-trove. It is vague and reminiscent. The original manuscript is in Chopin's handwriting; the piece was first played at the Chopin Commemoration concert in the autumn of 1894, at Zelazowa-Wola, and afterward at Warsaw by the Russian composer and pianist, Balakirev. This Nocturne was sent to his sister Louise at Warsaw in a letter from Warsaw, and was supposedly destroyed during the sacking of the Zamajski palace at Warsaw in 1863, but was saved and published. It is a romantic story, and true or not, doesn't much matter, because of the musical mediocrity of the composition. Is this the Nocturne of which Tausig spoke to his pupil, Rafael Joseffy, as belonging to the master's best period, or did he refer to the one in E minor?

James Huneker

Thematic Index.

À Madame CAMILLA PLEYEL.

Nocturne.

Larghetto. ($\bullet$ = 116.)

F. CHOPIN. Op. 9, Nº 1.

À Madame CAMILLA PLEYEL.

Nocturne.

F. CHOPIN. Op. 9, Nº 2.

À Madame CAMILLA PLEYEL.

Nocturne.

F. CHOPIN. Op. 9, № 3

À FERDINAND HILLER.

Nocturne.

F. CHOPIN. Op. 15, Nº 1.

À FERDINAND HILLER.

Nocturne.

F. CHOPIN. Op. 15, № 2.

Larghetto. (♩ = 40.)

5.

sostenuto.

leggiero.

con forza.

dolciss.

À FERDINAND HILLER.

Nocturne.

F. CHOPIN. Op. 15, N⁰ 3.

À la Comtesse D'APPONY.

Nocturne.

F. CHOPIN. Op. 27, № 1.

À la Comtesse D'APPONY.

Nocturne.

F. CHOPIN. Op. 27, Nº 2.

À Madame la Baronesse de BILLING, née de COURBONNE.

Nocturne.

F. CHOPIN. Op. 32, Nº 1.

Andante sostenuto.

9.

À Madame la Baronesse de BILLING, née de COURBONNE.

Nocturne.

F. CHOPIN. Op. 32, Nº 2.

Appassionato.

Nocturne.

F. CHOPIN. Op. 37. № 1.

Nocturne.

F. CHOPIN. Op. 37. No 2.

Andantino.

12.

dolce.

legato

À Mademoiselle LAURA DUPERRÉ.

Nocturne.

F. CHOPIN, Op. 48, No 1.

13.

À Mademoiselle LAURA DUPERRÉ.

Nocturne.

F. CHOPIN, Op. 48, Nº 2.

Andantino.

14.

À Mademoiselle J. W. STIRLING.

Nocturne.

F. CHOPIN. Op. 55, No 1.

À Mademoiselle J. W. STIRLING.

Nocturne.

Lento sostenuto.

F. CHOPIN. Op. 55, No 2.

À Mademoiselle R. von KÖNNERITZ.

Nocturne.

F. CHOPIN. Op. 62, Nº 1.

À Mademoiselle R. de KÖNNERITZ.

Nocturne.

F. CHOPIN. Op. 62, № 2.

18.

Nocturne.

Posthumous.

F. CHOPIN. Op. 72, № 1.
(1827)